New Trader 101:

The Fastest Way to Grow Wealthy In the Stock Market

By Steve & Holly Burns

Contents

Disclaimer:

This book is meant to be informational and should not be used as trading advice. All traders should gather information from multiple sources, and create their own trading systems. The author makes no guarantees related to the claims contained herein. Please trade responsibly.

When did I start trading?

Looking back at my life, I don't remember a time when I was not interested in the markets. As a teen, I was fascinated by compound return tables, and the magic of growing capital over time. Before the Internet, I remember looking at stock quotes in the newspaper, and my love for trading and the markets has only continued to grow.

I have spent the last 20+ years investing and trading. My drive to be a successful trader lead to reading hundreds of trading books and putting what I learned into action. Because the learning curve was so steep, I decided to create a shortcut for new traders; the kind of information I wish I could have studied when I was getting started. The New Trader 101 e-course and trading book is that shortcut. I have condensed all the key principles that a new trader needs to know into an easily understandable format. My goal is to get a new trader up to speed quickly, and trading successfully, with very little risk..

I hope you will join me as I show you how to build and grow your own capital, with low stress and minimal risk. It will most likely be one of the most rewarding things you ever do. It was for me.

-Steve Burns

stephen@NewTraderU.com

www.NewTrader101.com

What Students Are Saying

I thought about having a well-known, professional trader write the introduction for this companion guide, but I realized that this book is about you, the students that are devoting your time and energy to becoming better traders. I think it is more meaningful if you hear from a few of New Trader 101's successful students:

"I have spent over a year now in intense study of the market, charting, level 2, stock trending, options, technical and fundamental trading. Learned from books, various mentor-ship DVDs, webinars, and Internet videos. I was just going from on various trade to the next, most of the time losing more than I made. I have watched your e-course several times over the past few days. Since then, I have developed a rock solid trading plan. Anything I was having a problem with, I developed a set of rules to counteract it. Thank you so much for devoting your time to help new traders stay afloat in a sea that's filled with sharks! God Bless!"
–Jeremy C. Rhodes

"Steve has really outdone himself on this one, the value to cost of New Trader 101 is enormous. While putting the majority of focus on risk management, Steve also offers plenty of information concerning technical analysis. Steve has an incredible gift when it comes to explaining difficult to grasp concepts, and he frequently shares real trades while explaining the "why" behind the trade. The Pro Forum is very enlightening in the fact that you are able to learn from the questions of others, it is not unlike the learning platform of real colleges that offer online classes. I plan on renewing membership for many years to come."

–Jim Stewart

"After going through the e-course, I have gained more confidence to build my trading plan and actually trade the plan. The New Trader 101 Pro Forum is another great weapon to add to the arsenal. I've found the question and answer sessions really relevant, and the fact that I can create my own thread for my personal trading journal is really helpful. I got instant feedback from you as I was trading live! Now that's something. Thanks a lot!"

–Afif

"All your guidance has helped immensely. What I've learned has given me a foundation which will never leave me as long as I trade. The risk management portion of the trading system alone has already paid dividends. Any questions I have, you've been more than helpful answering or pointing out an article you've already written. Understanding the 'why's' of my trades has given me that 'care free state of mind'. Feels amazing. Thank you." –Fred Robles

Chapter 1: Mental Control

"Pride is a great banana peel—as are hope, fear, and greed. My biggest slip-ups occurred shortly after I got emotionally involved with positions." –Ed Seykota

The first step in a new trader's journey is overcoming their own emotional and mental saboteurs. Traders that can manage their emotions and control their ego, have a definitive edge over those who can't. One reason new traders can't make it through the first year, is that their trading decisions are based on subjective emotions instead of the objective realities of the markets. A trader can be their own worst enemy when their entry and exit signals are based on how they feel, rather than quantifiable data.

Ego

"Once you can learn that winning percentage doesn't really matter and throw your ego in the garbage…you will probably start doing a lot better." –Nial Fuller

Ego: a person's sense of self-esteem or self-importance.

A new trader must have competence before they have confidence: New traders with big egos always put confidence in their trading ability before developing competence in trading. Those that trade before educating themselves, are even ignorant of their own ignorance. Homework always comes before success. Traders can pay for their education by investing in study time, or if they choose to enter the markets before they are ready, they will pay other, more prepared traders.

Leave your ego at the door. Ego driven traders think they are special, and that they will beat the market with little effort. Despite having no winning trading record, too many have the hubris to think they are better than everyone else on the other side of their trades. Traders compete in the markets against other people; there will be hobbyists, but there will also many experienced professionals.

Stubbornness will get you nowhere. Stubbornness is simply the inability to accept mistakes, or to learn from them. A stubborn trader will lose money quickly if they are unable to accept that they made a mistake and refuse to cut their losses. Building capital is a result of being in losing trades for the shortest amount of time, while staying in winning trades for as long as possible.

Don't ignore risks. The reason most traders have an inflated position size, is that they ignore risk management in favor of confidence in an unknown outcome. This includes hoping against all logic that a trade will reverse. Simply realizing that any trade can be a losing trade, and using stop losses to limit the damage, will put a new trader ahead of many competitors.

Everyone needs a plan. Traders who nurture their own predictions more than they develop a robust trading methodology, will suffer the consequences sooner or later. There is no crystal ball, and trying to predict the future is a losing proposition. To be successful, new traders must realize that trading is about probabilities, trends, and risk management, not prognostication.

Trading is about being profitable, not being right. Ego driven traders put their desire to be right above their ambition of being profitable. When a trader caves to this kind of psychological sabotage, it is often a short trip to lost capital.

Egos make terrible traders. Don't put your desire to be right before your need for profitability. Successful traders follow a plan based on logic, reason, probabilities, historical prices, and risk management.

Greed

"Lesson number one: Don't underestimate the other guy's greed." – Scarface (1983)

Greed: intense and selfish desire for something, especially wealth or power.

Greed causes traders to trade too big and risk too much. Greed is the best get-broke-quick scheme available to traders. There are no shortcuts or secret strategies that will replace homework and the school of hard knocks. If you want to be successful, you need to focus on overcoming greed and the allure of easy money.

Greedy trading can result in blindness to danger, dizziness for profits, and a loss of trading capital. If I was a trading doctor, I would look for these eight symptoms before I made a greedy trader diagnosis:

Don't ignore the risks. Greed causes a trader to only look at things in reverse, by focusing on the best case scenario, and ignoring the worst case scenario. A trader must determine how much they can lose if the trade goes against them, and then be able to see the potential of subsequent trades.

Watch your position size. Greed causes traders to take too large a position size in hopes of scoring a big win. Profitability comes from consistently trading with an edge over time, not big trades that can just as easily turn into big losses.

Have realistic goals. A key to profitable trading is exiting a winning trade at a profit while the money is still there. Greed can cause a trader to stay in a trade too long with unrealistic expectations.

Trade with a plan. Greedy traders tend to enter positions on faith rather than quantified analysis, take trades where the odds are against them, and chase overextended trends. Greed for gain is a terrible entry method. Instead, develop and follow a robust trading plan.

Watch your longs. Greedy traders tend to enter long positions when a market is down 50% or more, believing they will double back and create a large gain. Positions have to be entered for a quantified reason, not out of greed.

Don't be tempted. Greed tempts a trader to enter the markets without doing the necessary homework. Traders entering the markets without doing the necessary research and developing a tested trading plan, will quickly discover their mistake.

Watch your odds. Successful traders act when the odds are in their favor, and not because they dream of enormous returns on any one trade. Buying far out of the money options, buying into a downtrending market before a reversal, and chasing an extended bull market, are all examples of entering due to greed.

Embrace experience. Greedy traders are looking for the easy path to money, and are not interested in hard work or gaining experience. Be prepared to put in long hours and treat trading just like any other business.

Don't succumb to the allure of easy money. Dedicate yourself to learning the market and developing a trading method that will return consistent, long term profits.

Fear

"The larger the position, the greater the danger that trading decisions will be driven by fear rather than by judgment and experience." –Joe Vidich

Fear is defined as a feeling of disquiet or apprehension. Trading with fear is a losing proposition, as it will inhibit your ability to enter a profitable trade, or cut a small loss before it becomes a big one. Fear generally comes from a lack of faith in your trading plan, or yourself. Here are a few ways that you can overcome fear.

Don't be afraid to lose on a trade. Traders fear being wrong so much they will hold a small loss until it becomes a liability. They will even add to the losing trade in hopes that it comes back. Never add to a losing trade. Don't be afraid of having a small loss. It is much better to cut your losses, than be wrong in a big way.

Don't be afraid to lose trading capital. New traders hate to lose money; they don't understand that 40-60% of their trades will be losses. Don't fear losing your capital so much that you can't take an entry. If you can't accept losses, you can't trade.

Don't fear losing potential profits. The fear of missing profits causes traders to chase a market trend far beyond the correct entry point and skews their risk/reward ratio. Trade at your system's proper entry point or secondary entry signal. Don't chase a market just because you are afraid to miss out on profits.

Don't fear your ability to maximize profits. If your rules tell you to get out of the trade, then exit. You must be disciplined about taking money off the table, and being greedy for that last few dollars could lead to major losses. Let your winners run but when the runner gets too tired to continue, bank your profits.

Fear can lead to bad decisions, on both ends of the trade. It can impair a trader's ability to take an entry signal and miss out on a winning trade, and it can limit their ability to let a winner run in order to collect all potential profit. Fear comes from a lack of faith in oneself, or in the chosen trading system. The only real fear a trader should experience, is the fear of trading before they are ready. Trading before developing a solid foundation of knowledge or a trading plan should scare any new trader.

What we learned

When you attain enough self-awareness to recognize and overcome the internal saboteurs ego, greed, and fear, your thoughts and actions will not be hindered by these destructive dispositions. You will be capable of making difficult decisions and implementing complicated strategies in any trading environment. You will attain an edge over your trading opponents, and increase your odds of becoming a successful trader.

NewTraderU.com blog:

Top Ten Side Effects of Greedy Trading

The Four Primary Trading Fears

A Trader's #1 Enemy is ....

Recommended Reading:

The New Trading For a Living

Chapter 2: Faith in Yourself

"If you want to make money in the markets, you have to build real faith in yourself as a trader, and believe in your winning methodology after doing the necessary homework." –Steve Burns

It is imperative that a new trader have faith in themselves and their trading plan. If you don't have confidence in yourself, you will be unable to implement your plan, or find trading success.

Believe in yourself. First, you must believe in your ability to follow your plan. If you don't have faith in yourself, fear will always undermine your confidence and success.

Do your homework. Successful traders create plans when the markets are closed, to give them clarity and guidance when the market is open. Creating a detailed plan in advance will decrease the risk of psychological factors negatively impacting your trades.

Make a commitment to your plan. New traders must commit to following their plan every day, regardless of how they feel, how much money they want to make, or their confidence in any single trade.

Be disciplined. Faith is built over time, day after day, by proving to ourselves that we will make the correct decisions. Discipline gives birth to confidence, which breeds success.

There is no such thing as a successful trader that lacks confidence in their abilities, or in their trading plan. By doing the necessary homework, creating a written trading plan, and being disciplined enough to follow that plan, confidence and success will follow.

Faith that you will take your entry signals

"There are just four kinds of bets. There are good bets, bad bets, bets that you win, and bets that you lose. Winning a bad bet can be the most dangerous outcome of all, because a success of that kind can encourage you to take more bad bets in the future, when the odds will be running against you. You can also lose a good bet, no matter how sound the underlying proposition, but if you keep placing good bets, over time, the law of averages will be working for you." – Larry Hite

Having confidence in yourself and your plan means that you will be able to take an entry signal when it is triggered. Open-mindedness is required, and uncertainty must be embraced; every trade has the potential to be a winner or a loser. It is important to understand that the outcome of a trade is not a reflection of whether you should have made the trade, it is a critical lesson in your growth as a trader.

Confidence in your entries

Don't be afraid to trade. No one can know the outcome of a trade. What we do know is that by following a plan, a trade can be a small winner, a big winner, or a small loser. Removing the possibility of a large losing trade from the outset, will help you make the trade with confidence.

Focus on quality. Focus on the quality of the execution of the trade. Take the signal when triggered. Don't front run or chase a trade after it is too late. The quality of your trade entries will have a large impact on whether you find success as a trader.

Be open to profits. Be ready to take the right entry. Failure to take entry signals based on your trading plan can cost you in the form of missed gains, regret, and loss of faith in your own ability to execute.

Stay true to your plan. Your trading plan is only as good as your ability to execute it.

Keeping an open mind, looking for good entries, and having the faith to execute those entries, will put you on the road to trading success. Embrace uncertainty and limit potential loss.

Experience

"If you can't take a small loss, sooner or later you will take the mother of all losses." –Ed Seykota

To be successful, you must learn to take your initial stop loss. Following this important rule will give you faith in your abilities. You will prove to yourself that you will always stop a small loss from becoming a big loss.

Keys to relying on your experience

Set your initial stop loss. It is crucial to set the stop loss at a price level that proves you were wrong about the trade. One of the biggest reasons for unprofitable trading is taking big losses when wrong. Know how much you are willing to lose and stick to it.

Don't let your ego get in the way. You must be able to admit that you're wrong. Learn to accept your loss, exit your trade gracefully when your stop is reached, and learn from the experience. Taking a stop loss can be painful and difficult to deal with, but taking a huge loss later will be much more difficult.

Go with the flow of the market. Don't become an anti-trend trader. Being stopped out many times can signal the beginning of a trend. As losses grow larger, you may be tempted to loosen your discipline. This will not lead to long term success.

Don't be afraid to take paper losses. This can be a large barrier for new traders, as they think that the loss doesn't count until they sell. The loss does count, and as it continues to grow, the lost mental and financial capital will take its toll.

What we learned

Conserve your time, emotions, mind, and capital by learning to cut your losses when you have been proven wrong. When you reach your initial stop, don't hesitate, get out and move on. There will be plenty of other trades .The art of the stop loss in trading is like the art of the fold in poker; it is the key to winning.

The art of the stop loss in trading is like the art of the fold in poker, it is the key to winning. Taking a stop loss when it is first hit can be painful and difficult. Taking a huge loss later can be much more painful and even more difficult.

NewTraderU.com blog:

Successful Trading: How to Put it All Together

The 17 Differences Between Good Trades & Bad Trades

7 Easy Steps to Blowing Up Your Trading Account

Recommended Reading:

Trade with Passion and Purpose

Chapter 3: Faith in Your Trading

"If you diversify, control your risk, and go with the trend, it just has to work." –Larry Hite

To be a successful trader, it is necessary to develop a methodology that you can believe in. By focusing on finding the right system that is customized to your needs and your lifestyle, you will build a strong foundation for trading success.

You should come to your trading with realistic expectations of annual returns and drawdowns. Your trading results will never come as a surprise when you understand the possibilities and probabilities of a particular system.

There are many trading methodologies, including trend follower, swing trader, macro trader, stock trader, and day trader. No matter how you decide to trade the market, your ability to make a profit will be determined by the edge for that specific methodology, and why it makes money over the long term.

A trading edge is defined as the positive statistical advantage that your trading system has when trading over time. It encompasses research, past profitability data, and position sizing parameters. Understanding your methodology edge will instill faith in your system, and allow you to trade confidently.

When it comes to a trading method, an edge is a system that has been defined and tested rigorously. It should make more money than it loses over time, giving the trader an advantage over the other market participants. This could be based on a study of past price action, technical indicators, chart patterns or many other quantifiable tests. The trader has to understand exactly why their methodology has a positive expectancy over the long term, so they can trade it with faith and confidence.

Four things that can help you find your edge:

-Historical entry points on chart patterns
-Using Technical indicators rather than opinions
-Trading a backtested system
-Letting winners run and cutting losers short
Understanding the edge for your preferred methodology is critical to determining if you will outperform other market participants and make money. This kind of research and preparation is necessary if you want to be successful.

Faith in your entries and exits

"Always know where you will get out even before you get in a trade." –Jack Schwager

Being able to act on entry signals when they are triggered, and exit a trade when you should, are the keys to successful trading. Without confidence in your plan and yourself, you will be unable to make the tough decisions necessary to manage winning trades. It is critical that you understand the potential outcome of every trade before you start.

Keys to executing with confidence

Trade with facts. A trader will gain confidence if they go into the trading day with quantified entries, rather than trading randomly based on opinions or emotions.

Limiting your losses. Understanding and embracing your exit plan if you are proven wrong will give you the necessary confidence to place a trade, because you realize your losses will be limited.

Have an exit strategy. Having a quantified exit strategy to lock in profits will take the stress out of the decision making process on when to lock in gains.

Embrace your plan. A trading plan is the new traders guide to having faith in their trading through every step of the process. Keeping an open mind, looking for good entries, timing your exits, and having the faith to execute those signals will put you on the road to trading success. Embrace uncertainty and limit potential loss.

Faith in your position sizing

Every trade should be: "Just a trade not a lifestyle change." –Dean Karrys

A profitable system can be turned into an unprofitable system through improper use of position sizing. A trader must structure position sizes in such a way that they can handle the mental, emotional, and financial stress.

Keys to profitable position sizing

Watch your stress level. If your emotions rise and fall with every tick of the price action, you are probably trading too large. Your trade execution should be emotionless.

Don't succumb to your own ego. Traders that trade too large will have trouble cutting their losses when the tide turns against them, due to the sheer size of the loss, and the finality of closing the position.

Don't ignore your plan. Trading with too much size causes a trader's emotions to become so loud that they are unable to hear their trading plan.

Stick to the facts. Position sizing is an exercise in mathematics. Avoid position sizing based on strong opinions and rumors at all costs.

What we learned

Faith in trading is developed over time, by focusing on developing your system, managing emotions, and controlling self-doubt. By studying methodology, entries and exits, and position sizing, a new trader can trade confidently and successfully.

NewTraderU.com blog:

<u>7 Ways to Trade with an Edge</u>

<u>10 Things a Trader Can Know</u>

<u>The 5 Faiths Needed for Trading Success</u>

Recommended Reading:

The Inner Voice of Trading

Chapter 4: Stress Management

New traders quickly discover that there is a big difference between reading books or trading in a simulated account, and trading with your own money online. The ability to manage stress is critical to the long term success and happiness of a trader.

Trade size

"Risk no more than you can afford to lose and also risk enough so that a win is meaningful." –Ed Seykota

New traders run the risk of exhausting their emotional reserves by consistently trading uncomfortable position sizes. There is a real danger of losing emotional capital as well as financial capital when you trade outside your comfort zone. Trading is a business, not an amusement park ride. If you find yourself with white knuckles, just trying to hold on, you need to re-examine your trade size.

How to avoid emotional ruin

Remain emotionally neutral. Your trade size should be one that does not elicit any emotional response. If you experience increased heart rate, this is a warning that you are trading outside your comfort zone. Ignoring the warning signs can lead to a damaged psyche and the inability to place trades in the future.

Learn your comfort zone. Don't rely on what others tell you; only you can know what you feel comfortable trading. The best mathematical risk level may be higher than you feel comfortable risking. How much you choose to risk is in your control, and this is an effective way to manage stress.

Choose the right trading vehicle. Trading stress can vary based on the trading vehicle. Trading in a stock market index like the Dow Jones Industrial Average may not create much stress, but the volatility of trading a growth stock may cause too much stress for you to handle as a new trader.

Start small. Start out by trading small, regardless of your access to trading capital, and increase your trade size as your comfort and confidence grows. Don't trade with a large account until you are a seasoned trader with a tested method, fully developed trading system, and a detailed trading plan.

Don't run the risk of experiencing emotional ruin and cutting your trading career short. Decrease your position sizes until your stress levels on entry become completely manageable, and don't interfere with your ability to follow your trading plan in a relaxed, and disciplined manner.

Risk exposure

"That cotton trade was almost the deal breaker for me. It was at that point that I said, 'Mr. Stupid, why risk everything on one trade? Why not make your life a pursuit of happiness rather than pain?" –Paul Tudor Jones

The total risk exposure to your account will have a direct impact on your stress level and your quality of life. Avoiding elevated levels of risk will increase your chances of success and preserve your peace of mind.

Limiting your risk

Don't overreach. Even if each trade is small, ten open trades, each risking 1% of your total trading capital, has the potential to cause a large, single day drawdown. Try to limit your risk by not spreading yourself too thin.

Diversify your positions. If you are holding ten long stock positions, a bearish stock market could bring them all down together. Hold uncorrelated positions in different markets like currencies, precious metals, oil, and stocks that do not usually move in the same direction, to reduce risk and stress.

Check your plan. You will decrease your stress if your plan is meeting your expectations. Make sure that you feel comfortable with your buy points, and that you fully understand the trading vehicle. Each position should be in something that has been researched and planned carefully.

Watch your mood. Your total risk exposure to all open trades should never change your mood or your quality of life. If you are unable to sleep because of your trading choices, you need to re-examine your plan.

By limiting your risk of exposure, you will increase your winning percentage and assure a high quality of life. Longevity in trading is much more important than short term gains. Manage stress and risk so you can trade for many more years to come.

Personality

'If I try to teach you what I do, you will fail because you are not me. If you hang around me, you will observe what I do, and you may pick up some good habits. But there are a lot of things you will want to do differently. A good friend of mine, who sat next to me for several years, is now managing lots of money at another hedge fund and doing very well. But he is not the same as me. What he learned was not to become me. He became something else. He became him." – Colm O'Shea

Most new traders are looking for a magic pill. They ask questions like, "What is a profitable trading method that can make me a lot of money?" Instead, they should be asking, "What is a profitable trading method that fits my personality, that I can trade long term?" The type of person you are will help determine what kind of trader you become, and this will affect your stress level on a daily basis.

The four types of traders

Conservative trader. Conservative traders seek consistent and predictable returns with minimum draw downs and screen time. Risk management is their top priority. They will take less return in exchange for less drawdowns. They trade small and focused in the markets they are experts in. These are the traders content with 15% - 20% annual returns.

Aggressive trader. Aggressive traders want big returns and they are willing to take on risks that have the highest probabilities of success. They love taking trades and are active with entries and exits, trading across a variety of markets. They enjoy screen time, volatility, and fast moving markets, and like to leverage options and futures. These discretionary traders often become millionaires, but they are also the ones that blow up their trading accounts.

Quantitative trader. Quantitative traders love to back test systems and study historical price action. They focus on what can be measured and quantified. They believe in a purely mechanical system, with computerized market models and signals based on past price history. They love historical data and statistics.

Perfectionist trader. Perfectionist traders hate to lose any money. They love high winning percentages, and cut their losses very quickly. Most of them gravitate to day trading for the quick results, potential for high winning percentages, and small losses. They may have difficulty holding a position for longer than a few days.

What we learned

If your system does not fit your trading personality, then you will be in a perpetual state of stress trying to trade it. The biggest question is "Can you trade the system you want to trade based on its time frame, required screen time, and projected stats?"

NewTraderU.com blog:

Top 15 Ways to Manage Trader Stress

10 Ways to Manage Trading Stress

10 Tips for Managing Trader Stress

Recommended Reading:

Mastering Trading Stress

Chapter 5: Capital Preservation

"Where you want to be is always in control, never wishing, always trading, and always first and foremost protecting your ass. That's why most people lose money as individual investors or traders because they're not focusing on losing money. They need to focus on the money that they have at risk and how much capital is at risk in any single investment they have. If everyone spent 90 percent of their time on that, not 90 percent of the time on pie-in-the-sky ideas on how much money they're going to make. Then they will be incredibly successful investors." –Paul Tudor Jones

A trader's focus above all else should be to not lose money. If your #1 priority is to manage risk, you will have more success with setups and entries, you will stop chasing profits, and you will begin to grow as a trader.

Always focus first on what you can lose, rather than what you could gain. Follow this simple principle, and good things will follow. Become a risk manager and you will limit your drawdowns, preserve your trading capital, and avoid ruin.

Be your own risk manager

Prepare for the worst. First, you need to think about what will happen if this becomes a losing trade. Review your stop loss and position size, and don't anticipate potential profits.

Survive your loss. All traders have losing streaks, the question is whether or not you are trading in a way that will enable you to survive the streak. Analyze the percentage of trading capital you are risking per trade, and see how many consecutive losing trades you can survive. Making adjustments to your trade size during losing streaks is crucial to your success.

Stay grounded. Don't fall prey to unrealistic expectations. There will be many hard knocks and painful losses between you and consistent profit.

Plan. Plan. Plan. Under no circumstances should you take impetuous trades based on a hunch or rumors. The only way to control the risk of ruin and enjoy a long and profitable trading career, is to develop a plan and follow it.

Good traders are risk managers, first. They control their risk of ruin, limit their drawdown, and avoid getting into trouble by placing big trades that erode their trading capital and confidence.

The difficulty of drawdowns

"At the end of the day, the most important thing is how good are you at risk control." –Paul Tudor Jones

A drawdown is a normal occurrence for a trader. The key to surviving a drawdown is staying disciplined in your entries and exits, and not trying to change your system or trading plan when things get rocky. A drawdown in trading capital does not mean that your trading system doesn't work. Believe in yourself and stay the course.

Keys to surviving drawdowns

Evaluate your position sizing. During difficult market environments or losing streaks, it is time to trade smaller. Consider cutting your position sizing in half (or less) until the environment improves. Don't make poor choices in a desperate attempt to recover losses.

Understand the math. Once capital is destroyed, it takes a much larger return to get back to even. If you have $10,000 and lose $1,000, that is a 10% drawdown. However a 10% return on your new trading capital does not get you back to even. That takes you back to $9,900, and now you need an 11.1% return to break even.

Watch your step. As your drawdowns deepen, it becomes more difficult to climb back out, both financially and emotionally. Your top priority as a trader is managing your risk in your individual trades, and your total capital.

Be prepared for a losing streak. If you are in pursuit of high returns, then you can expect drawdowns that are about half your return rate. If you maintain consistent position sizing, you will be safe from the risk of ruin. The question is: "Where will your account be with a string of 10 consecutive losses?" Some traders will be out of business, others will be down 10% from their equity peaks. How you handle drawdowns through disciplined trade execution, position sizing, and managing losses, will be a key component to your ultimate trading success.

Pressure

"Losing a position is aggravating, whereas losing your nerve is devastating." –Ed Seykota

Never underestimate the mental and emotional pressure that losing money can put on a trader. Those that are able to manage their egos and self-worth in the midst of losing, are the traders that are built for this stressful business.

Keys to keeping cool

Cut your losses. Losing trades that are getting worse are a major cause of pressure. Cutting a loss will ease your stress, and will allows you to look at the trade with an unbiased perspective.

Don't overexpose yourself. If you limit your open trades, based on your current entry signals, you can focus on markets that are more familiar, and limit the risk of waking up to big losses across several positions.

Know when to get in and out. When you enter a trade with no stop loss, you have the potential for an unlimited ruin. Trading with no stop loss is like driving a car with no red lights.

Uncertainty is the ultimate stressor.

Trade for the right reasons. You have to trade based on the market's price action, and not because you need money. The pressure to trade to pay bills can cause desperation that leads to very costly errors. Trading is not a job with a regular income, the wins and losses are randomly distributed over time.

Mental and emotional pressure can put a trader at a serious disadvantage and cost them their edge. Knowledgeable traders will be able to control their losses by knowing when to exit a losing position, and are more likely to find long term success.

What we learned

Risk management is the most important aspect to study as a new trader. Learn to trade for the right reasons and limit drawdowns, and you will avoid ruin and preserve your trading capital. Successful risk management will separate you from your competitors.

NewTraderU.com blog:

Why BIG trades are a BAD idea

A Trader's Downward Spiral

Be a Trader Not a Gambler

Recommended Reading:

Come Into My Trading Room

Chapter 6: Risk / Reward

"There's no reason to take substantial amounts of financial risk ever, because you should always be able to find something where you can skew the reward risk relationship so greatly in your favor, that you can take a variety of small investments with great reward risk opportunities that should give you minimum drawdown pain and maximum upside opportunities." – Paul Tudor Jones

Trades that have the potential to be big wins or small losses is an important element that is often overlooked. Inexperienced traders will endanger their accounts by chasing hot stocks, trends, and chart patterns without considering the importance of controlling risk. Large losses will quickly dwindle a trader's account, and small wins will do little to pay for those losses.

Successful trades have to be asymmetric, where the downside is carefully planned and managed, but the upside is open ended. This is a crucial element for trading success, and has to be understood, planned for, and carefully executed.

Keys to risk/reward ratio

Do the math. The ratio is calculated mathematically by dividing the amount of profit the trader expects to have made when the position is closed (the reward), by the amount the trader could lose if they are stopped out for a loss.

Understand your odds. Understand that even the best traders only win about 50-60% of the time. No one is perfect.

Analyze each trade. Ask yourself if each trade has the potential to either be a big win, or a small loss. There should be no other accepted outcome for any trade.

Cut your losses. Constantly remind yourself that cutting losses quickly will be the key to your success. Having a plan with a clear exit strategy will save your capital and your sanity.

In order to trade confidently and win 50-60% of the time, a trader must carefully analyze their trades by accurately calculating their risk/reward ratio, and be disciplined enough to stick to their plan, no matter what.

Win rate vs. risk/reward Ratio

"It's not whether you're right or wrong that's important, but how much money you make when you're right and how much you lose when you're wrong." –George Soros

The bigger your winning trades, the lower your win rate must be to become profitable. You don't have to be right all of the time, you just have to be right big, and wrong small.

Risk/reward facts

-With a 1:1 risk/reward ratio and 50% win rate a trader breaks even.

-With a 2:1 risk/reward ratio and about a 35% win rate a trader breaks even.

-With a 3:1 risk/reward ratio and about a 25% win rate a trader breaks even.

The key to discovering your risk/reward ratio is to first determine where price has to go to show you that you are wrong. This is usually the key support level, and what you use to place your stop loss. Your potential profit target will be set as a rally to a key resistance level or a new all-time high. Remember that your stop loss level is your risk, and your target is your reward. Allowing one of the two to play out is the key increasing your odds of profitability.

Asymmetry

"....Asymmetry allows you to be confident about what is wrong, not about what you believe is right." –Nassim Nicholas Taleb

High winning percentages are difficult for many traders, especially with tight stop losses. It is a much simpler path to profitability, to capture the majority of trends in your trading time frame, instead of trying to be right about every entry. A great formula to use is a 3:1 risk/reward ratio.

Keys to 3:1 risk / reward ratio

Know the upside. Know how much you will risk on any one trade, and then don't enter a trade where the upside is not at least three times your risk of loss, if your stop is hit.

Measuring risk. Understand that with a 3 to 1 ratio, you can risk 1% of your trading capital for the possibility of making 3% of your capital in profits.

Cutting your losses. You can cut losses before your stop is hit, but you must allow enough room for normal fluctuations and volatility. Use position sizing that you are comfortable with in proportion to your trading account.

Let your winners run. Allow winners to run as far as possible with the use of trailing stops. You never know when you will have a big win, with the right entry and trend.

A great formula to use is a 3:1 risk/reward ratio, with this ratio a trader is risking $100 to make $300. If 100 shares of stock are bought for $30 a share and the stop is at $29 then the stock should only be purchased if it is probable that the stock could run to $33 based on the chart pattern or back tests. At a $33 share price profits could be taken or ideally if it runs to $34 a trailing stop could be set at $33 to give the stock an opportunity to be an even bigger winner but set the trailing stop to lock in the $3 per share gain. After ten trades your account could look like this:

Lose $100

Make $300

Lose $100

Make $300

Lose $100

Make $300

Lose $100

Make $300

Lose $100

Make $300

Profit $1,000 with only a 50% win rate!

However if you allow losers to run hoping they will come back so you can take profits on a rebound then you can get into trouble fast.

What if the stock you were trading fell from $30 to $29 and you didn't stop out and it kept falling to $20? What if you started wanting to lock in profits at $31 and not let your winner run to capture the full profit potential? The dynamics of your risk/reward ratio would change leaving you unprofitable even though you had an 80% win rate.

Lose $1000

Make $100

Lose $500

Make $200

Make $100

Make $100

Make $200

Make $100

Make $100

Make $100

Lost $500 even with an 80% win rate!

Other ways to measure the ratio:

In trades you can also plan to cut your losses if the stock drops 5% while taking entries on stocks that can run 15% of more. Of course ideally you would only want to use 20% of your trading capital on one stock so a 5% drop in the stock would only be a 1% loss of total trading capital.

Another way to measure a 3:1 ratio is that you can risk 1% of your trading capital for the possibility of making 3% of your trading capital in profits.

Remember that you can cut losses even shorter if you are proven wrong before your stop is hit, but at the same time you have to allow enough room for normal fluctuations and volatility in your stop and use position sizing that you are comfortable with for your trading account size. I also recommend you to allow winners to run as far as possible with the use of trailing stops. You never know when you could have a huge win with the right entry and trend.

First know how much you will risk on any one trade then do not enter a trade where the upside is not at least three times your risk of loss if your stop is hit.

What we learned

It is not the winning percentage of a trader that determines their profitability but the size of all their winning trades versus the size of all their losing trades. This is the math that determines profitability. The fastest path to profitability is to trade with a process that maximizes winning trades and minimizes the losing trades.

NewTraderU.com blog:

Asymmetric Trading

Why Big Wins and Small Losses = Profitability

Expectancy

Recommended Reading:

Trend Commandments

Chapter 7: The 1% Rule

"The very first rule we live by is: Never risk more than 1% of total equity on any trade." –Larry Hite

One of the simplest lessons to ensure long term success, is to never risk more than 1% of your trading account on any one trade. Often dismissed as being too conservative, use of this rule will eliminate the risk of ruin and create a solid foundation for all trading success.

The Confusion

The 1% risk management rule does not refer to a 1% price movement in what you are trading as your stop. It also does not refer to trading with 1% of your total trading capital as a position size for a trade. The 1% rule means that you never lose more than 1% of your total trading capital, by implementing proper stop loss and correct position sizing on each trade.

Keys to Understanding the 1% Rule:

Eliminates the risk of ruin. The key to proper risk management is adjusting your stop losses and position sizes based on the volatility of your trading vehicle, so that when you are wrong, the consequences are only 1% of your trading capital.

Lowers your stress. Using the 1% rule lowers your stress level and allows you to think clearly, acting on actionable data, rather than ego, fear, or greed.

Limits losses. The reality is that you will have 10 or more losing trades in a row, or one unexpected event that causes a large loss. By using the 1% rule, you will survive these difficult times.

Preserves your capital. The #1 job of a new trader is not to trade aggressively, but to protect their capital so it can grow. Managing your risk by implementing the 1% rule is the quickest and easiest way to accomplish this.

Traders should not confuse the 1% rule as limiting their ability to make money. Even though the stop loss is set at 1% of your trading capital, your win size is unlimited. 1% maximum losses on your trading capital, with 3% returns on half your winning trades, will make you profitable.

Big trades are not better

"I try very hard not to risk more than 1% of my portfolio on a single trade. –Bruce Kovnar

Only risking 1% per trade will limit your trading size and enable you to sidestep big losses. The 1% rule causes proper position sizing and good placement of stops, and it will lower your stress when the trade is moving strongly for, or against you.

1% rule in action

1% risk per trade is the beginning point for position sizing:

Figure out what is 1% of your current trading capital, and decide where your logical stop loss is for your trade; the price level where you will know that you were wrong after a loss of a key support, resistance level, or trend line. The amount of the distance between your entry, and your stop loss, is your start for position sizing.

For example: If you are trading a $100,000 account and an Apple trade entry is the break of the 50 day moving average at $100, then the stop is a 5% drop below your entry. $5 is the distance of the risk. So if $1,000 is my 1% risk, and I am risking $5 a share, then $1,000 divided by $5 is 200 shares. This is my position size. If I am wrong, and the price drops below $95, then I must exit with a $1,000 loss. The trade should be taken with the potential of a move to $115, based on the current trend or chart pattern, to create a 1 to 3 risk/reward ratio.

The danger of ignoring the 1% rule, is that if you are risking 5% or 10% of your capital on any one trade, and you are risking a equal weighted 5%, if you lose 10 times in a row, you are down 50%. You will have to see a 100% increase just to get back to even.

Trading 1%

"By risking 1%, I am indifferent to any individual trade. Keeping your risk small and constant is absolutely critical." –Larry Hite

If you are risking only 1% of your capital on each individual trade, then each one should only be one of the next 100. Embracing this philosophy will allow you to trade in the right frame of mind, with no emotions or ego.

Keys to trading 1%

Know your ratio. The 1% is the designation of how much trading capital you will have at risk, and your position size will be determined by the volatility and average trading range for your trading vehicle.

Understand the volatility Stock trading in an index will allow for larger positions than in speculative or volatile growth stocks. Small positions in volatile stocks increase your probability of being able to hold them longer; avoiding noise and capturing a trend.

Don't stray from 1%. It may be tempting to increase your rule to 2%, but this should be avoided. Many professionals risk only half a percent to limit drawdowns.

Watch correlations. If you have ten open trades and all ten go down at the same time, you will have a drawdown of 10% in one day. Limit your correlated open trades in order to reduce drawdowns. This is a compliment to the 1% rule.

The 1% risk rule is used to determine position sizing, based on the price level of the exit and how much the trader will lose if the exit is triggered. It is critical to the preservation of capital, and necessary to increase the confidence and survival of new traders.

What we learned

The 1% rule is one of the most misunderstood rules in trading, and leads to confusion for many new traders. To the uninitiated, this rule may seem too conservative. However, by limiting your losses to only 1% on any one trade, you preserve your trading capital, and even after a losing streak, you will live to trade again.

NewTraderU.com blog:

5 Quick Tips for Risk Management

10 Reasons Risk Management is Essential

Risk Management in 1 Lesson

Recommended Reading:

The New Market Wizards

Chapter 8: The Risk of Ruin

"It does not matter how frequently something succeeds if failure is too costly to bear." – Nassim Nicholas Taleb

Risk of ruin means losing all your trading capital, making the odds of getting back to where you started, almost zero. How you manage your capital will determine your success more than your entries and exits. Never put yourself in a situation where you will have a large drawdown, or give back all your recent trading profit, in one day.

Money management

"The key to long-term survival and prosperity has a lot to do with the money management techniques incorporated into the technical system." –Ed Seykota

The majority of new traders risk too much. Although you may have a big win, you will eventually give back your profits and destroy your trading account. Learn to manage your money and you will have a significant advantage over other traders.

Keys to managing your money

Guard your profits. All the money in your trading account should be closely guarded to insure continued growth. You must trade all of your capital inside a winning system, using a trading plan and proper risk management. Don't play fast and loose with your profits.

Don't gamble. Trading outside your plan is gambling, and you will eventually give back those profits. Only trade within your system and continue to build your trading capital.

Honor the 1% rule. Never risk more than 1% of your trading capital on any one trade, and you will limit your risk exposure, and improve your odds of success.

Watch for a better edge. Experience will show you how to position size the best trades with the most capital, and lesser trade setups with smaller position sizing. This will make your best trades your biggest winners, and decrease your odds of losing.

Managing your trading capital is mandatory for a profitable trading career. By learning to stick to your trading plan, limiting your losses, and seeking a competitive edge, you will continue to grow your capital and trade for years to come.

Surviving a losing streak

No one likes to think about it, but it's going to happen. You will experience a losing streak at one point or another in your trading career. This happens to everyone, even the greatest traders in history have had to recover from the emotional and financial damage of a losing streak. But with proper planning, and risk management, you can limit your losses and bounce back quickly.

5 Questions to ask yourself

"Where will your account be with a string of 10 consecutive losses?"

"Is the trading system valid? Have enough backtests or chart studies been completed to show it is a winning system in the historical context of the markets? Is the system the problem?"

"Did I follow my trading plan 100%? Were some of my losses due to a lack of discipline in entry, exit, or position sizing? Is my discipline the problem?

"Do I know how many losses my system will have with my winning percentage expectations?"

"Are my losses due to a changing market environment? Has the market changed from trending to range bound, or has it grown volatile?"

Be indestructible

"Where you want to be is always in control, never wishing, always trading, and always, first and foremost protecting your butt." –Paul Tudor Jones

Insulate yourself from loss and make yourself indestructible by following these money management techniques:

-Never lose more than 1% of your total trading account on any one trade. All losses must be small losses.

-Only hold three positions at any one time. Your maximum portfolio heat should be limited to a 3% loss at one time, if every position goes against you simultaneously.

-Hold uncorrelated assets to reduce your correlated risks. By having positions in different asset classes like commodities (energy & precious metals), currencies, and stock indexes.

-Incorporate rules into your trading plan that promote smaller trades during losing streaks. For example, after four losing trades in a row, you may risk only a half percent of trading capital by cutting your position size in half. Trading the smallest during losing streaks can reduce your drawdown dramatically.

When a trader starts to lose money in trade after trade, it is crucial that they ask the right questions and make the right decisions to protect their capital.

What we learned

When trading over your maximum position size, your chances of being profitable when trading on one idea, one market, or one trade, is almost zero. Learning to manage your risks, rebound from losing streaks, and insulating yourself from costly losses will make for a much more enjoyable and profitable trading experience.

NewTraderU.com blog:
Solve These 5 Problems Right Now
The Risk of Mental Ruin
Turkeys and Risk Management
Recommended Reading:
A Trader's Money Management System

Chapter 9: Time Frame

"The answer to the question 'What's the trend?' is the question 'What's your time frame?" –Richard L. Weissman

A new trader has to decide what time frame they will trade before building their trading plan and developing their system. Each time frame has a unique use of charts, entries and exits, as well as support, resistance levels, and breakouts. As a new trader, your goal should be to understand and apply winning principles for your chosen time frame.

Day trading

Day traders buy and sell on the same day, and close out all positions when the market closes. They do not carry any positions over into the next day. Day traders attempt to profit on the price moves that happen in one day, using intra-day charts to capture intra-day trends. This is a very time consuming time frame because most day trading systems require being in front of the computer at least eight hours a day to be available to take all entries and exits as they are triggered. This time frame is one of the most stressful due to the speed of the entries and exits and the instant feedback of wins and losses in trading capital. Day traders are said to sleep like babies because they have no overnight risk with a position moving against them. However, they can also miss out on strong trends that occur mostly with gaps at the open and outside of the intra-day chart.

Day trading is not for people with day jobs due to the need for constant attention and monitoring of price action. It can give a new trader a lot of experience, and quickly build up a record of trades to analyze. This time frame is well suited for those that love making fast decisions and receiving immediate feedback. Day trading is generally not for those that enjoy a more low-key approach.

Key price levels and indicators for day traders

-Opening price

-First hour break outs of the daily range

-Daily high and low price

-Setups from the daily chart

-Price reaction to news events

-Intra-day moving averages of price

-Intra-day oscillators

Swing Trading

Swing traders want to buy low and sell high, and this is a method that many traders are comfortable using. Swing traders buy and hold their positions over multiple days or weeks. This works best in markets that have defined price ranges. The key to swing trading is buying support and then selling into resistance in an up-trending market, on a short time frame. However, they may also go short into resistance on the daily chart.

Swing traders carry positions overnight and are subject to gap ups and gap downs outside of the previous day's trading price range at the market open. They also can benefit from morning gaps if positioned in the right direction. Since swing trading is mainly done off the daily chart, it is much easier for traders with jobs to trade this time frame, as most trades can be completed at the market open or close.

A swing trader's edge is that they buy dips to support levels when others are selling out of fear. They also sell short into resistance levels when others are buying out of greed. Swing traders do best in range bound markets with well-defined support and resistance levels. They do not do as well in trending markets that are making higher highs and higher lows, with no pullbacks. Swing traders can be profitable in trends by finding key pullback levels, or by using oscillators like the RSI.

Trend Following

The key to trend following is having trades positioned on the right side of the market, over the long term. Trend followers create systems for longer time frames. They also sell short positions in markets that are trending down. Trend followers use different signals and technical indicators to quantify possible trends, like the 50 and 200 day moving averages. Some also use weekly charts and 10 week and 40 week moving averages for trend identification. The key for trend followers is to stay on the right side of a trend, for as long as possible.

A trend follower's edge comes from the use of reactive technical analysis to capture long term trends in financial markets. By using quantified, back tested signals from a diversified watch list of asset classes, they trade price action. Trend followers tend to have low winning percentages, but small losses and large winning trades over time. Trend following is for long term capital appreciation of money, and is usually not suited for those that are trying to trade for a living, or need high winning percentages and consistent profits with minimal drawdowns.

Trend following only requires trading at the end of the day or the end of the week, in most cases. Because it requires less monitoring, this time frame generally affords the best quality of life. However, those thinking of following this time frame should be interested in doing a lot of research and backtesting of past market action, to understand the probabilities of trends occurring in the future.

Position Trading

Position traders enter and exit long term trades in the markets over weeks, months, or in some cases, even years. They usually build positions based on a theory, or for fundamental reasons, and have a long term thesis that they are waiting to see play out in the price action. Position traders may use weekly charts, or may trade strictly off fundamentals.

Position trading is usually based off a forecast or prediction about the future movement in price of an asset in comparison to where it is in the current moment. Position traders may think that a commodity is too high or too low, and begin to build their position in the belief that in a specific time frame, it will move to their target price. Position traders rely on their convictions, banking on the asset being profitable when their price target is reached.

Position trading is best left to the very patient, and those that want to express their long term convictions, while waiting for their positions to come to fruition.

Stock Trading

While stocks can be traded in all time frames, someone that trades stocks exclusively is usually trading them for the long term. The stock's growth is based on the future potential of the company. Most stock traders are stock pickers and look for the companies whose growth will drive up the stock price after each earnings announcement. Most stock traders will trade a stock off the daily and weekly chart, and hold it as earnings expectations push the price higher. This takes time: weeks, months, and sometimes years. However, you can choose to trade stocks on a shorter time frame using price action, and short-term moving averages.

Stocks provide both opportunity and risk as they tend to trend well and be volatile. A stock can move faster and farther than other trading vehicles because it is a representative of a company, and is not a diversified asset. News, earnings, and changes in the company itself can send stocks up or down quickly, with little warning.

To increase your odds of profitability, you should make sure that you purchase the right company, at the right time, for the right price. Here are key things a stock trader needs to look for:

Key indicators for stock traders

-Current earnings should be greater than the previous quarter. Ideally, a trend of increasing earnings over the past year should be present.

-A company with an innovative business model that is a 'game changer' can be a big winner.

-Buy the leader of an industry. You want to own the best, because that is where the professionals will be looking to buy.

-Do not buy stocks during a downtrend. Bear markets and downtrends tend to bring down all stock prices as investment capital exits the stock market as an asset class.

What we learned

The same principles apply to all trading time frames, and money can be made on any time frame by following a winning trading system, with discipline, while managing risk. You should choose which time frame best fits your lifestyle and personality.

NewTraderU.com blog:

5 Trading Timeframes

Moving Average Answer Key

The Anatomy of a Trader: Holding True to Your Trading Time Frames

Recommended Reading:

Short Term Trading

Chapter 10: Trading Plan

"If you can't measure it, you probably can't manage it... Things you measure tend to improve." –Ed Seykota

The thing that sets profitable traders apart, is that the winners focus on facts, current price reality, and historical context, while others base trading decisions on feelings, beliefs, and opinions.

Subjective: *Based on or influenced by personal feelings, tastes, or opinions. Proceeding from or taking place in a person's mind rather than the external world.*

Subjective traders are intertwined with their trades. They generally enter out of greed and exit based on fear. They believe in their opinions more than the reality of price action, and how they feel about a particular market. Being right and gratifying their ego may be more important to them than being profitable.

Objective: *(Of a person or their judgment) not influenced by personal feelings or opinions in considering and representing facts. Having actual existence or reality.*

Objective traders have a quantified method, system, rules, and principles they trade by. They know where they will get in a trade based on facts, and where they will get out based on price action. Objective traders have a written trading plan to guide them. They react to what is happening in quantifiable terms, following the flow of price action, and not the flow of internal emotions.

Questions to ask before you make your plan:

-What exactly is your entry signal going to be? What price action or technical indicators will trigger you to enter a trade? Entry signals can only be created based on backtesting or chart pattern study over a large data sample.

-What is the risk/reward ratio for the trade you want to take? How much are you willing to risk if the trade is a loser and your stop is hit? How much could you make if you are right? Is it worth it in terms of risk and stress?

-What are the probabilities that this entry will be a winning trade based on past historical price data and charts? With the winning percentage in mind, how big do the winners have to be and how small do you have to keep the losers for the trading system to be profitable?

-Where should your stop loss be? At what price level will your entry be wrong and signal you to exit the trade with a loss? Do not put stops in obvious places; move them outside possible intra-day noise.

A successful trading plan

"The single trait that makes most people fail as a trader is their lack of discipline in devising a trading plan and following their trading plan." –TheStockTradingZone.com

Successful traders create a plan that puts the odds of winning in their favor, while gamblers take random trades, hoping they will win based on luck. Trading randomly comes from a trader's ego; they believe they are smarter than other traders, even though there is no proof based on past performance.

Components of a trading plan

Entering a trade: You must know at what price you plan to enter your trade. Will it be a break through resistance, a bounce off support, a specific price, or based on indicators? You need to be specific while trading your system in real-time, using entries to maximize the probability for potential gains.

Exiting a trade: At what level will you know you are wrong? Define your exit strategy for losing trades: a loss of support, a specific price level, or a stop loss? Know where you are getting out before you get in. Always start with your stop placement.

Position sizing: You determine how much you are willing to risk on any one trade before you decide how many shares to trade. How much you can risk will determine how much you can buy based on the trading vehicle's price and volatility in relation to your stop loss level.

Money management: Never risk more than 1% of your total capital on any one trade.

Regardless of how you trade, everyone must have a plan to have a chance at success. Great traders have great trading plans.

Building your own plan

"Traders must find a methodology that fits their own beliefs and talents. A sound methodology that is very successful for one trader can be a poor fit and a losing strategy for another trader.' –Jack Schwager

Many new traders entering the trading game can't get the right answers because they aren't asking themselves the right questions. Much of the success traders experience is attributable to how well they know themselves. Only after you honestly answer these questions, will you have enough self-awareness to be a successful trader.

-What markets will you trade? Futures, options, equities, or forex? You must fully understand the markets you choose, the leverage, the liquidity, and their nature to trend our stay range bound on your time frame.

-What are your entry parameters? You need setups and entry signals that are proven to be profitable through price and chart studies.

-How will you exit a winning trade to lock in profits? Money is only made in the exit. Trailing stops and profit targets enable you to exit a winning trade while the money is still yours to take home.

-What is your edge over other traders in the market? If you can't answer this question, you need to find an advantage before you place your next trade.

What we learned

Your success as a trader will depend on how well you mitigate losses to your trading capital. Don't get caught up in daily trading results. If you ask the right questions, and then go seek out the answers, the only barrier between you and success, is time.

NewTraderU.com blog:

10 Things Traders Must Quantify

A Trading Plan: Do You Have One?

10 Things a New Trader Should Know From the Start

Recommended Reading:

Survival Guide for Traders

Chapter 11: How to Trade

"The 10 day exponential moving average (EMA) is my favorite indicator to determine the major trend. I call this "red light, green light" because it is imperative in trading to remain on the correct side of a moving average to give yourself the best probability of success. When you are trading above the 10 day, you have the green light, the market is in positive mode and you should be thinking buy. Conversely, trading below the average is a red light. The market is in a negative mode and you should be thinking sell." –Marty Schwartz

Entry signals

"Look for low risk, high reward, high probability setups." –Richard Weissman

Trading is about finding ways of quantifying and identifying the trend in your time frame and capturing profits by being on the right side of it. The true definition of a trend is higher highs and higher lows or lower highs and lower lows. You only need to find a few tools that fit your own trading methodology and goals.

Breakout indicators: A trader can enter based on a breakout of a key price level, a trend line break, a moving average, or a chart pattern.

Support: Support is a price level on a chart that reflects the lowest price in a time frame. When buyers are ready to purchase an asset for a specific price, they cause that price level to hold. Support is the lowest price level that an asset can travel before no one is willing to sell it at a lower price.

Resistance: Resistance is a price level on a chart that has been the highest price in a time frame. Sellers are ready to exit or sell an asset short, and cause that price level to hold. Resistance is the highest level that people are willing to buy at that price.

Breakouts: Breakout trading is when you buy or sell at the beginning of a new price range, as the old one has broken through a loss of support, or a breakout above resistance.

Homework: An entry signal must be based on how it performed in the past, or after studying historical charts to identify and quantify previous success rates.

Probabilities: The larger the sample size of past data on the entry setup, the better the odds are that the setup has statistical validity. Testing hundreds of examples is a great place to start.

Stock trading: Stocks trend based on their future earnings expectations, and the level at which they are being accumulated or distributed. Growth stocks go through phases of accumulation due to earnings expectations, and the purchasing power of mutual funds and money managers. Stocks also go through stages of distribution, as earnings disappoint and trend down.

Different environments: It is crucial to test how your entry system performs in different types of market environments. Markets in uptrends, downtrends, those that are range bound, or volatile, will produce different results. Understand that the market environment will change your system's performance.

Trends are caused by the cycles of accumulation and distribution of asset classes by investors and traders in pursuit of returns on their capital. The economics of supply and demand is the primary driver of prices in financial markets.

Exit strategy

"Decide where you will get out before you get in." –Jack Schwager

High winning percentages are difficult for many traders, especially with tight stop losses. It is a much simpler path to profitability to capture the majority of trends in your trading time frame, instead of trying to be right about every entry. A great formula to use is a 3:1 risk/reward ratio.

It is not your entries that make you money, but how you manage your exits that will determine whether a trade is profitable. Your winners will have a window of opportunity to lock in profits. Your initial stop loss is your bodyguard against big losses.

If you're wrong: When you enter a trade you must also identify the price level that invalidates your entry. Your stop loss level has to be set outside the range of ordinary price noise that occurs in your own time frame.

If you're right: If the trade trends in your favor, you need a plan for locking in profits. A trailing stop is used by raising your initial stop loss, as the asset trends in your favor. Trailing stops can be moved to a previous day's low-of-day, or a short term moving average.

The key to this strategy, is to exit based on the price action that is in place. After your entry, your exit parameters must be planned and managed just like your initial entry. You must have a plan to get out if you are wrong, and a plan to lock in profits if you are right, before you ever enter a trade. Limit your losses when wrong, and let your winners run.

Position sizing

"Traders focus almost entirely on where to enter a trade. In reality, entry size is often more important than the entry price." –Jack Schwager

The total dollar value of the asset being traded is your position size. The percentage of capital the trader is willing to lose, and the correct location of the stop loss, will determine position sizing.

If you position size correctly, then no single losing trade will ever be more than 1% of your total trading capital. For example: If you need to determine position size for a trade from a $100,000 account, a 1% of capital at risk gives you $1,000 as your maximum loss if you are wrong.

If the trader wants to trade the $SPY and their entry signal is a break over the 50 day simple moving average at $200, and their stop loss is a 2% loss of the 50 day back to $196, with a loss of $4 a share then the trader can trade 250 shares of $SPY.

$100,000 Account

1% Risk = $1,000

Stop Loss of $4 to $196

Position Size will be 250 shares at $50,000.

We calculate the position size by taking $4 as the dollar stop and dividing by $1,000 as our maximum loss, this equals 250 shares. If each share losses $4 the total loss would be $1,000. The stop is based on the 50 day being lost by 2% of the asset to prove to the trader that the 50 day break out signal failed.

$200 - $196 = $4 divided by $1,000 = 250 shares

Risk exposure: To manage drawdowns most effectively, a maximum of three trades should be open at any one time. This will limit your losses due to price reversals or shock events, and make your equity curve much more manageable. You can adjust total positions to fit your own parameters for annual returns and your tolerance for drawdowns. You can also increase positions during markets more favorable to your trading system.

Volatility: Base potential stop levels on the previous ten days trading ranges. If you are trading a stock with $5 average daily trading ranges a position size of 200 shares for a $100,000 trading account would be the maximum position sizing you could use to avoid the daily price noise if you are trying to capture multiple day trends.

The formula is: Position Size = (TTC * %TTC) / SV

TTC is Total Trading Capital
%TTC is the percentage of total capital to risk per trade.
SV is the stock's volatility (10-day Average of the true range).

What we learned

Your ability to correctly and consistently implement your entry signals, exit strategy, and position sizing will determine your success as a trader.

NewTraderU.com blog:
ALL Types of Traders are after the SAME thing……
7 Good Ways to Exit a Trade
Trading: The Difference Between Playing Offense & Defense
Recommended Reading:
How to Make Money in Stocks

Chapter 12: The Mechanics of Trading

"The essential element is that the markets are ultimately based on human psychology, and by charting the markets you're merely converting human psychology into graphic representations. I believe that the human mind is more powerful than any computer in analyzing the implications of these price graphs."–Al Weiss

While fundamental analysis is the study of a markets potential value, technical analysis is the study of the behaviors of the participants trading in that market. Investors are focused on valuation metrics for an asset, while traders primarily trade price action.

Your goal as a trader is to develop ways to capture trends inside your timeframe through quantified methods, based on proven principles, and backtested market studies.

Price behavior is the best guide for entries, exits, position size, and showing the actions of buyers and sellers in the present moment.

Price is the result of an agreement between the buyer and the seller at any given moment in time. Your purpose is to be on the right side of a market, as it is being accumulated or distributed, inside your time frame.

Price is the result of an agreement between the buyer and the seller at any given moment in time. Your purpose is to be on the right side of a market, as it is being accumulated or distributed, inside your time frame.

Keys to profitable trading

Being profitable is the result of making better decisions than the majority of your opponents.

Some quantifiable signals for entering trades:
-Price breaking above or below key moving averages on charts
-Price breakouts beyond established price ranges
-A chart pattern breakout
-A break above or below the previous day's high or low
-Trades based on technical indicators like the RSI or MACD
Possible ways to place stop losses after entry:
-A key moving average does not hold as support or resistance for price
-A breakout trade returns back into the previous trading range
-Price reversal back inside the chart pattern
-A reversal back under the previous day's low or above the previous high
Potential ways to set a trailing stop:
-Use a close below the previous day's low for long positions
-Use a close above the previous day's high for short positions
-Use a short term moving average breach like the 5 day, 10 day, or 21 day

Momentum trading, trend trading, and swing trading

Momentum trading, trend trading, and swing trading are three ways to capture profits by trading price action.

Momentum trading

Momentum entry signals are based on the beginning of a strong breakout of a short term trading range. Momentum trades are higher highs or lower lows on a chart based on a new trading range. Momentum is usually a short term trade. Momentum traders are looking to capitalize quickly on a strong move.

Momentum trade: Amazon

This is an example of momentum as Amazon gapped up after their earnings announcement. The stock moved up $25 a share after its opening day gap low.

A momentum trader would have captured some of this move, by buying into the gap at the end of the day, on the day of the gap.

Gaps have to be given time to prove they will hold. Momentum traders can use the low of the first day as their stop loss level. Moving your trailing stop to a close below the previous day's low each day, is one way to trail a winning trade and eventually lock in profits.

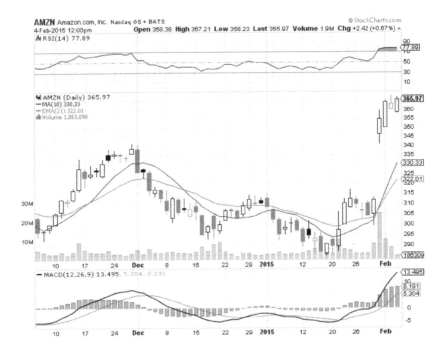

Trend trading- A trend trade is when you enter the market's trend of higher highs and higher lows, or lower highs and lower lows in your time frame. Trends can also be measured by moving averages that are going higher or lower on the chart.

Trend trade: $USO

Many traders wanted to go long oil, although there was no signal to do so on the daily chart. $USO made consistently lower highs and lower lows for months, over multiple day periods. In this example, the 21 day EMA was a great filter to show the trend as it acted as overhead resistance, showing the actual trend with its down slope. The longer term 50 day moving average also confirmed this. The best course of action in this market, was to sell short on all time frames on most days.

Swing trading

Swing trading is the art of buying low and selling high, or in some cases selling short at high prices, and buying back at lower prices. The buy level for swing traders is the expected price support area, and they generally plan on selling into resistance. Swing trading works best in markets that are range bound, and have defined support and resistance levels. Support is measured by its ability to maintain buyers at those price levels. Be aware that the more times a support or resistance price level is tested, the greater the odds that it could be broken, and start a trend.

Swing trade: Amazon

On three different occasions, and over the course of several months, Amazon found buyers at the $285 price level. Support is the price level where buyers that have been sitting on the sidelines decide that they will get back in. They begin accumulation, while sellers have refused to sell below that level. The tide begins to turn, as willing buyers and sellers will not sell at lower prices.

Moving averages, chart patterns, and technical indicators

Moving Averages, Chart Patterns, and Technical Indicators are tools used to capture price action in a trader's time frame.

Moving averages

"The 10 day exponential moving average (EMA) is my favorite indicator to determine the major trend. I call this "red light, green light" because it is imperative in trading to remain on the correct side of a moving average to give yourself the best probability of success. When you are trading above the 10 day, you have the green light, the market is in positive mode and you should be thinking buy. Conversely, trading below the average is a red light. The market is in a negative mode and you should be thinking sell." –Marty Schwartz

-A simple moving average (SMA), is indicated by a line on a chart, based on the calculation of the average price of a trading instrument, over a set time period.

-An exponential moving average (EMA) gives greater weight to recent prices, to make it more reactive to price action.

-Moving averages are powerful tools, and they show key levels for support, resistance, and entry and exit signals. They act as an unbiased trend indicator, while trend lines are subjective, moving averages are quantifiable.

Moving averages- 21 Day

The 21-day moving average commonly marks the short-term trend, the 50-day moving average the intermediate trend, and the 200-day moving average denotes the long-term trend of the market.

The 21 day moving average will act as a filter for price action, keeping a trader on the right side of a short term trend. The higher the volatility, and increased daily price range, the less useful a short term moving average becomes. As you can see, above the 21 day EMA would keep you on the right side of the market action, as it trended both down and then up.

The next step is developing a way to lock in profits as the trend over extends beyond the moving average. This can be accomplished by adding an oscillator to lock in profits near the 30 RSI, signaling oversold.

Moving averages - 50 Day

The 50 day moving average allows a trader to capture a trend for months. This moving average can also acts as a key support level during bull market pullbacks. Monster stocks are often accumulated by money managers at this level.

Moving averages- 200 Day

The 200 day moving average allows trend followers to capture long term trends over the course of a year. This is the ultimate dividing line between Bear Markets and Bull Markets. Major downtrends tend to happen after prices drop below the 200 day moving average. One of the first signs of the start of a Bull Market is price breaking and closing above the 200 day moving average. The price in relation to the 200-day moving average is a signal of whether we are in a bull or bear market cycle.

Generally speaking, bulls trade the long side above the 200-day moving average, while bears like to sell short when price is below it. Bears usually win and sell into rallies below this line, and bulls like to buy into pullbacks above it. This line is one of the biggest signals in the market telling you which side to be on. Many long term trend following systems use this as a primary long term indicator, across different markets.

Moving averages- 40 Week

An alternative way to capture trends, is to trade the long term time frame with a 40 week moving average. It is very similar to the 200 day moving average, but is calculated on a weekly basis. To use this, multiply the time frame on a daily chart by 5 to see what moving average is similar to it on the weekly chart. (5 days X 40 weeks = 200 days). There are trend followers that make trading decisions once a week based on this formula.

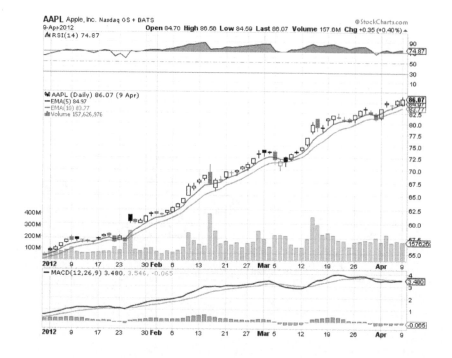

In a strongly trending market that has great momentum, the 5 day
EMA or 10 day EMA can act as an end of day support level for
weeks and months. In up trends this is caused by heavy
accumulation of an asset by the majority of market participants and
large money managers. Apple was being accumulated in 2012 by
many money managers and the public and closed above the 10 day
line for months.

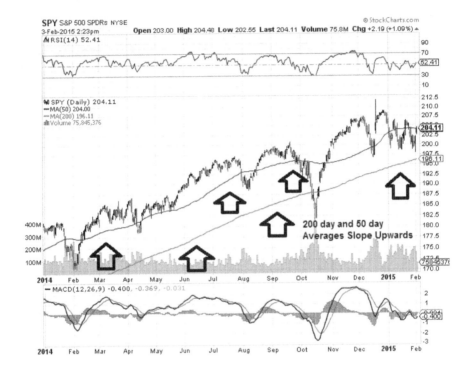

Some traders watch for when a moving average in their time frame begins to slope upwards or downwards and consider it one indicator of a trend beginning, continuing, or changing. As you can see the 200 day and 50 day moving averages both slope higher as the long term uptrend is in place with higher highs and higher lows.

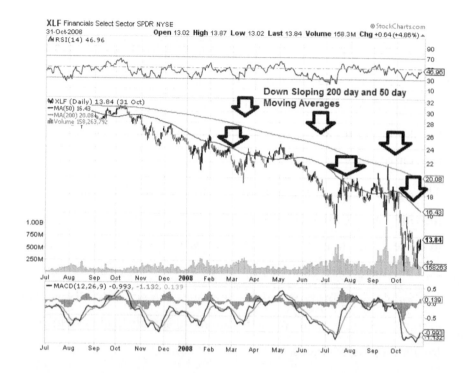

Both the 200 day and 50 day were sloping down in the financials in 2007 and 2008 indicating heavy distribution.

Moving average crossover systems

Some traders use systems that give buy and sell signals when a shorter term moving average crosses over a longer one. Legendary trend trading pioneer Richard Donchian used a five and twenty day moving average crossover system for buy and sell signals.

One systematic way to use moving averages as trading signals and smooth out entries and exits during volatile periods, is to develop trading systems using moving average crossovers. Using two moving averages, you can create buy signals that are triggered when the shorter term moving average crosses over the longer term moving average.

The exit or sell short signal is triggered when the shorter term moving average crosses back underneath the longer term moving average. Your trading time frame and backtests determine which moving average best suits your trading vehicle, time frame, and methodology. Short term moving averages can generate false signals before catching a trend, and generate more signals than systems with longer moving averages.

Longer term moving average crossover systems can give back profits before the exit is triggered. The underlying principle is that you develop a moving average crossover system that enables you to have big wins and small losses that allow profitability. The purpose of moving average crossover systems is to replace opinions and predictions with a quantifiable way to capture trends.

Moving averages can be used to build profitable systems for capturing trends and can help guide your entries and exits. Moving averages are a good way to quantify what is actually happening, and can replace your subjective opinions with facts.

Chart patterns

When I got into the business, there was so little information on fundamentals, and what little information one could get was largely imperfect. We learned just to go with the chart. Why work when Mr. Market can do it for you? – Paul Tudor Jones

Chart patterns

A chart pattern is created by mapping out prices on a chart in graphic form. Chart patterns are identified by lines connecting price points: closing prices, highs, or lows over a specified time period. Chartists attempt to identify the patterns in market participant buying and selling behavior. Chartists study these patterns to identify emerging trends. The study of chart patterns is one path to understanding technical analysis.

Trend lines

Trend lines are the primary building blocks of chart patterns. Chart patterns are designed with straight lines that are used to connect multiple price points on a chart, reflecting ascending or descending highs and lows in price, over a time frame.

Trend lines must start from left to right on a chart, and must be straight and intersect through at least two points. Signals are created as a trendline is broken. Straight horizontal trend lines on a chart show support and resistance levels. Diagonal trend lines connect higher highs or lower lows, and show up trends and down trends based on their slope.

Chart patterns are primarily used as trend breakout indicators as an entry signal, as price breaks out of their trendline. Here are a few examples of entry signals:

Here is the simplest resistance and support chart pattern. Support was tested three times but held. This is a range bound chart. It failed to break above resistance on two attempts and finally broke out on the third try.

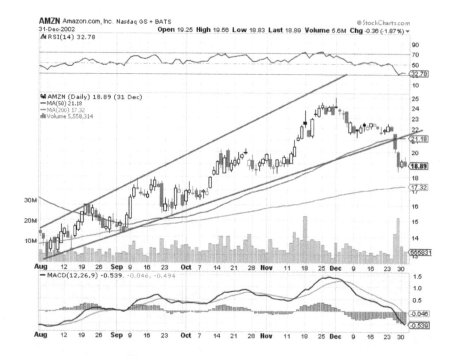

Ascending channel pattern

This is an ascending channel pattern. The top trend line is created through higher highs and the bottom trend line shows higher lows. This is a simple chart pattern showing an uptrend in this stock. The break below the lower supporting trend line is the signal for a potential exit of the long position, and/or the possibility to sell short due to the trend break. You will notice the loss of momentum and the move away from the top trend line toward the end of the move.

Descending channel pattern

This is a descending channel pattern created by lower highs and lower lows. The gap up and break out above the upper trend line shows the end of the descending pattern, and the potential for a first try at a bottom in the price, and the attempt of a reversal.

Exits- The exit after a chart breakout will determine the profitability of the trade. Trailing a stop loss using a short term moving average, a stop loss with a close below the previous day's low, or having a price target, are three ways to exit with a profit after a good entry. There is a lot of art to the science of trading chart patterns. To put it simply, chart patterns are quantifying breakouts of price ranges, giving a trader the potential of capturing a trend.

Technical indicators

"A technical indicator offers a different perspective from which to analyze the price action." –StockCharts.com

Technical Indicators are derivatives of price action that are used to give an added dimension to analyzing the potential meaning of a chart. A technical indicator's value is computed by applying a specific formula to the price data of a trading vehicle. They offer an additional angle that helps to analyze the price action. The prices used to compute different technical indicators can be based on the open, high, low or close over a specific time frame.

There are a few indicators that use closing prices only, and there are some that measure the momentum of a trend, or whether a market is likely to be oversold or overbought after a lengthy run. They are used as tools for trading price action, whether to confirm the direction of a market, or to be used to measure the potential end of a trend. Technical indicators can be used in conjunction with studying past price patterns on charts, and during backtests.

RSI

The RSI is a technical momentum oscillator that compares the amount of recent gains to recent losses to try to read the overbought and oversold levels of a market's price action. The RSI has a range of 0 to 100. A market is supposed to be overbought with a reading of 70. For traders, this is an indication that it may be time to sell their long positions at this level. The RSI at 30 is supposed to signal that an asset is starting to be oversold, and may present a good risk/reward ratio to go long at that level.

Center line crosses at the 50 can be used as the beginning of a trend in the direction of the break (+50 bullish / -50 bearish). The traditional use of the RSI for swing trading is best used in stock indexes. The 65-70 range indicates overbought and time to exit longs. The 30-35 range indicates oversold and a potential buy signal. The RSI oscillator works best for swing trading in range bound markets. It does not work well for indicating extremes in trending markets, as higher highs or lower lows happen for extended periods.

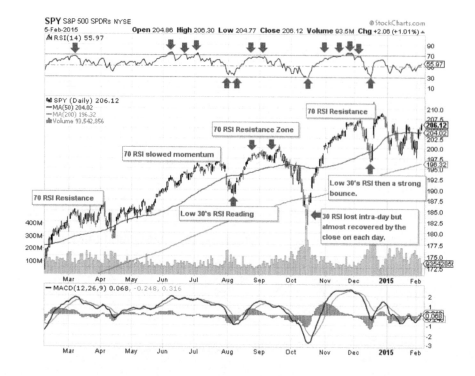

In the S&P 500 index, the RSI is a useful tool in addition to moving averages and price trends. The stock market as a whole tends to revert to the mean as opposed to trending strongly for an extended period of time. There are always buyers of stocks as an asset class that want to invest in companies. Company buybacks add to the support of price levels. Over long periods of time, the $SPY ETF seldom goes far above 70 RSI on the daily chart, and usually recovers the 30 RSI before the close of the trading day.

This can give traders of $SPY an understanding of where the risk/reward begins to shift against them, if they are long near the 70 RSI, or short near the 30 RSI. It also gives a level to trade against when taking longs in $SPY at the 40 RSI or 35 RSI. At these levels, you have great odds that the 30 RSI will hold as it is rarely broken over long periods of time. The 70 RSI is a great indicator of slowing of momentum with an increased chance of a pullback, rather than momentum building fast enough to bring it to 80 or 90 RSI. The RSI is a great oscillator tool for swing trading range bound markets and can also be used as a momentum indicator in markets that tend to trend.

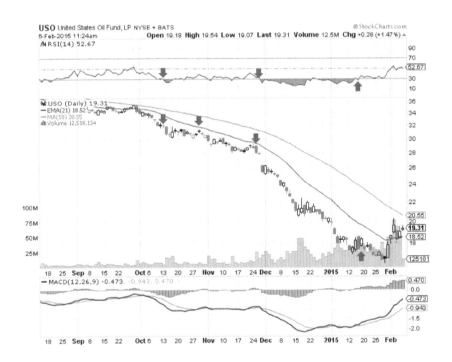

Commodities tend to trend strongly based on supply and demand levels. In this chart, the 30 RSI loss is a breakout to the downside momentum signal to go short as a new downtrend was beginning. The 21 day and 50 day moving averages confirmed the trend. Even in historically range bound markets, breaking below the 30 RSI is a signal that a big downside trend could emerge.

With individual growth stocks, the 70 RSI can act as a breakout momentum indicator.

In this chart, you see that Apple broke out above the 10 day EMA, then the key resistance level, and finally the 70 RSI. Any of these three breakouts could have been a signal to go long on this chart. The trailing stops could have been a loss of the 10 day EMA, or a drop back below the 70 RSI as examples of trade management.

RSI is not a standalone signal, and has to be used as one tool among many. It will give you an indication of an extended move that could reverse or strong momentum. Never trade using RSI until you have studied the historical charts of the markets you intend to trade, or backtested the indicator on historical price data.

The MACD

This is a technical indicator that attempts to measure momentum of a markets price action. It converts two moving averages into two lines on a chart by subtracting the longer term moving average from the shorter term moving average. The MACD shows the relationship between two moving averages.

The formula the MACD uses to calculate its lines comes from the 26 day exponential moving average, and the 12 day exponential moving average of a market. The 26-day EMA is subtracted from the 12-day EMA to create a line. Then the 9 day EMA of the MACD is placed with the sum of the first lines to create signals for entries and exits based on crossovers. The second line is used as a signal line as it crosses over the first.

MACD is about the relationship between two intermediate term moving averages. Its signals are based off of convergences and divergences of these moving averages. The convergence of its lines, indicates the likelihood that a market is in a trading range. A divergence of the two lines as they move away from each other occurs during trends in that market.

The MACD is primarily used for trend trading signals on crossovers of the MACD line over the signal line. The MACD is not useful for identifying overbought and oversold markets as it is a measurement of convergence and divergence of two moving averages around a '0' line.

The MACD also has a histogram in the indicator box along with the two lines. The histogram is calculated by subtracting the 9-day EMA line from the MACD-line. The slope of the histogram above or below the '0' line is a sign of the trend of the market. The histogram above zero shows upwards momentum and below '0' shows downtrend potential.

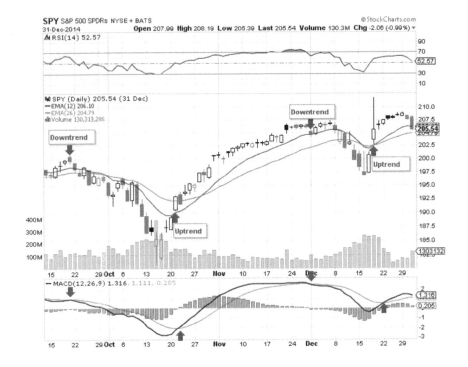

The indicator box below the chart shows the black MACD line crossing over the red signal line to create entry and exit signals. This chart shows the power of simple MACD crossovers for capturing short term swing trades on the $SPY chart. The MACD crossover gives faster signals than the moving averages themselves do in most cases. The MACD is just one trading tool, and the RSI indicator could have helped with a better exit as the short term trends became overbought or oversold.

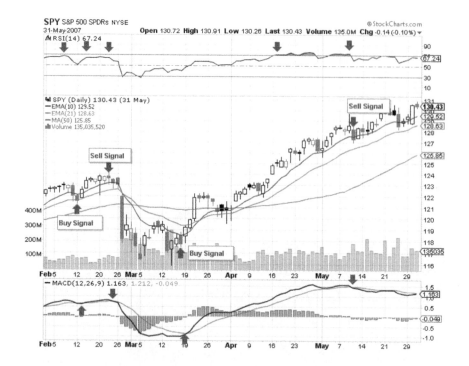

In this chart, we see how the MACD as a standalone indicator captured several momentum swing trades. The MACD works best in markets that have trends. It can capture momentum trends longer than RSI as it begins to signal overbought. MACD is a great tool to have in a trader's toolbox, and can be used with other signals for a well-rounded trading system.

A trader should consider these quantifiable indicators when beginning to build a trading system:

- The price range inside their time frame
- Previous days price range
- Trend
- The chart pattern
- Support

- Resistance
- Moving averages
- RSI
- MACD

NewTraderU.com blog:

10 Great Technical Trading Rules

John Murphy's Laws of Technical Trading

Moving Average Answer Key

Ten Rules for Trading Pocket Pivots

How I Like to Trade Bullish Gap-ups

Cup and Handle Chart Patterns

Steve Burns
New Trader U

Want to learn more?

In the New Trader 101 e-course, you'll get:

-13 high quality videos covering how and why to trade

-Real trade examples with detailed charts

-An active member forum with hundreds of ongoing conversations

-A live Q&A session with Steve every week!

Visit http://www.newtraderu.com/new-trader-101-signup

and join other traders just like you!

Did you enjoy this book? Please consider writing a review!

Read more of our titles:

Moving Averages 101

New Trader Rich Trader

New Trader Rich Trader 2

Show Me Your Options!

Made in the USA
Coppell, TX
19 November 2022

86625014R10056